Property of
Peter & Adrienne
do not
steal !

Clueless George
Goes to War!

Clueless George Goes to War
copyright August 2005
Pat Bagley
All rights reserved
Printed in the United States
editor: Dan Thomas

9 8 7 6 5 4 3

ISBN 0-9744860-5-1

White Horse Books
1347 S. Glenmare St., Salt Lake City, UT 84105
(801) 556-4615

Clueless George
Goes to War!

Pat Bagley

White Horse Books

This is George.

George is a monkey.

George is the president.

George is a good monkey.

George lives with The Man.

One day George heard a big BOOM!

"What was that?" asked George.
"Saddam has attacked America," said The Man.
"Are you sure?" asked George.
"No, but it's convenient," said The Man.

"What should we do?" asked George.

"This is war," said The Man. "We must send an
army to kill evil and destroy badness.

And while we're at it, we must also
secure our strategic access to a
quarter of the world's
known oil reserves."

"Do I get to dress up?"
asked George brightly.

"Sure," smiled The Man.
"You're the boss."

Outside, the people were frightened and angry.
"Bad men have killed our sons and daughters and husbands and wives!" the people said. "Those bad men must be stopped!"

"I will smoke out those bad men," said George.
"I will smoke them out of their holes, dead or alive!"
"Hooray!" said the people.

So George went to war.

He got to push little
armies around on
a big board . . .

He got to fly
in a jet . . .

He got to dress up . . .

George even got to declare victory!

And when it was all over . . .

But that was the curious thing —
it wasn't over.

BOOM! BOOM! BOOM! went the improvised explosive devices.
BOOM! BOOM! BOOM! went the car bombs.

Apparently, the people who George beat in the war were
cheaters and didn't know they were beat.

This made George mad.
Furious George said to all the bad men,
    "Bring it on!"

So the bad men, who didn't know that
George was only speaking rhetorically, said,
    "Okay. Let us bring it on."

Soon, everything was a bloody, gory, horrific mess.

BOOM! BOOM! BOOM!
   went the car bombs.
BOOM! BOOM! BOOM!
   went the suicide bombers.
BOOM! BOOM! BOOM!
   went the IEDs.
BOOM! BOOM! BOOM!
   went the retaliatory strikes.

"Whew!" said George.
"This is hard work!"

Then the people came running up.

"George! What are you doing?!!" they said.
"The bad men who attacked America—they
aren't there. You invaded the wrong country!"

The Man whispered
in George's ear.

"If you are not with me,"
said George, "then you are
with the bad men."

"But, but, but . . ."
stammered the people.

The Man whispered in George's ear again.

"How dare you say our brave troops are fighting
in a wrong war! That PROVES that you
are with the bad men!"

"But, but, but," sputtered the people. "What about the missing WMDs? What about the 'fixed' intelligence? What about the missed signals that warned of an attack ahead of time?

What about the terrorists who actually planned and executed the attacks on us? What about invading a country that didn't attack us? What about the lack of accountability? The botched planning? The official lies? What about the billions and billions and billions going to your friends at Halliburton and the other billions and billions and billions going to your other friends in the oil business? What about the way America's image has been dragged through the mud? How do we patch up things with countries that used to be our friends? What about the official policy condoning torture? And the practice of imprisoning people without a hearing? What about the thousands of young Americans who are dying? And the tens of thousands who are being maimed? What will happen to them? Shouldn't we be building a better country here at home instead of halfway across the world?"

"I AM A WAR-MONKEY PRESIDENT!!!"

said George, without any prompting from The Man.

"YOU ARE ALL MISLOYAL DISASSEMBLERS!"

And for good measure, The Man added,

"Go f*** yourselves!"

Just then a boy stepped out from the crowd.
"Hey, Mr. Man!" he said.

"What do you want?" said The Man.

"Mr. Man," said the boy,
"there's something you
 should know."

"What's that?"
 asked The Man.

"Your monkey is naked!"
  said the boy.

At first the people just stared.

Then someone giggled.
        Someone else snorted.
                Soon, they were all laughing
                so hard their sides ached.

"He's naked!" they all said. "He's just a little, naked monkey!
Why didn't we see it before?"

Everyone thought it was hysterical, except for The Man,
who was busy punching a number into his cell phone.
        "Homeland Security? This is The Man—we have
        a situation here . . ."

That night, as The Man tucked him into bed, George asked,
   "Why couldn't they see my Commander-in-Chief
      War-monkey outfit?"

"They were obviously America-hating, evildoer-loving liberals,"
The Man patiently explained.

"So that's
why you sent
them all to
Geronimo Bay. . ."
mused George.
"Shouldn't we
have given them
trials?"

"The answer to
that is very
nuanced,"
said The Man.

George furrowed
his brow in thought.
"I don't do nuance," he said.

"Exactly," said The Man. "Don't worry about it."

And George didn't.

The End

About the Author

Pat Bagley is an award-winning editorial cartoonist from Utah—the same state, by the way, which gave Bush his biggest margin of victory in the 2004 election. Bagley's work has appeared in *Time*, *The Guardian of London*, *The Los Angeles Times* and *The National Review*. He is also the author of *101 Ways to Survive Four More Years of George W. Bush*.